Orlando
MAGIC

BY JIM GIGLIOTTI

Published by The Child's World®
1980 Lookout Drive • Mankato, MN 56003-1705
800-599-READ • www.childsworld.com

ISBN 9781503824584
LCCN 2018964285

Printed in the United States of America
PA02416

ABOUT THE AUTHOR

Jim Gigliotti has worked for the University of Southern California, the Los Angeles Dodgers, and the National Football League. He is now an author who has written more than 100 books, mostly for young readers, on a variety of topics.

TABLE OF CONTENTS

GO, MAGIC!

The history of the Orlando Magic is full of ups and downs. The Magic began play in 1990. The team was pretty good pretty fast. Then came a period of **drought**. That was followed by some good years again. Now the team is back at a low point. That can only mean one thing for Magic fans. The good times are sure to come back soon!

Nikola Vucevic slams home a basket for the Magic.

Jonathan Isaac is one of the young players hoping to bring the Magic to the top.

WHO ARE THE MAGIC?

The Magic play in the NBA Southeast Division. That division is part of the Eastern Conference. The other teams in the Southeast Division are the Atlanta Hawks, the Charlotte Hornets, the Miami Heat, and the Washington Wizards. The Magic have finished in first place five times in their history. They have made the **playoffs** 14 times.

WHERE THEY CAME FROM

Orlando and Miami are two of the biggest cities in Florida. Both cities wanted an NBA **expansion team**. The league couldn't decide which one would get it. The NBA thought long and hard about it. In the end, the league figured both cities should have a team. The Miami Heat began play in the 1989 season. The Orlando Magic started the next year.

Scott Skiles was a key part of the Magic from 1989 to 1994. He later became an NBA coach.

9

Mo Bamba throws down a dunk in a game against Southeast Division rival Miami.

WHO THEY PLAY

The Magic play 82 games each season. They play 41 at home and 41 on the road. They play four games against the other Southeast Division teams. When Orlando plays Miami, it is called the Sunshine State **rivalry**. The Magic also play 36 games against other Eastern Conference teams. They play each of the teams in the Western Conference twice.

Orlando is the home of Disney World. The city is home to the Magic Kingdom theme park. Many fans suggested the name Magic for the city's new basketball team. It is a **unique** name. No other pro sports team ever had the name. The Magic play their home games at the Amway Center. The 2012 NBA All-Star Game was played there.

The Amway Center is in downtown Orlando. During games, team mascot Stuff the Magic Dragon performs (left).

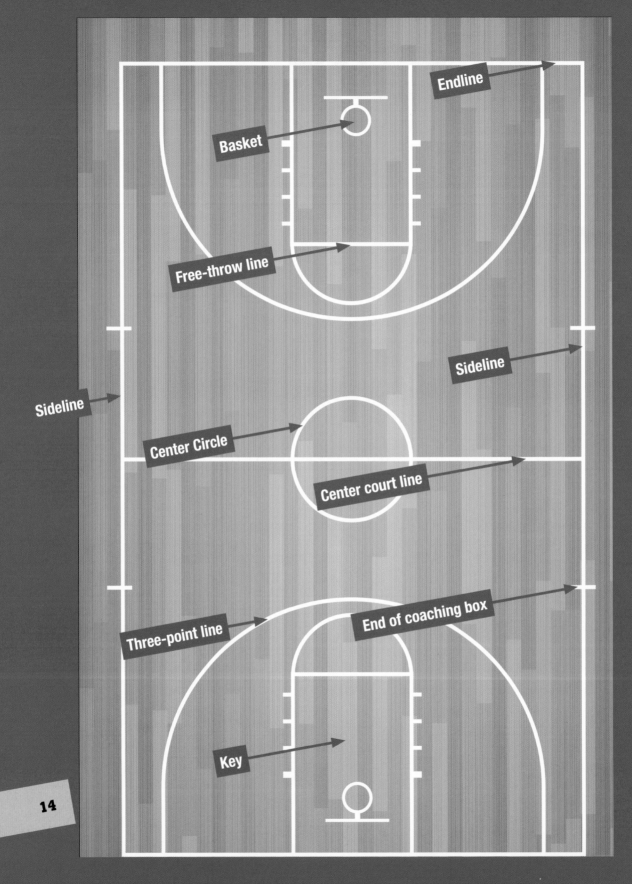

Endline

Basket

Free-throw line

Sideline

Sideline

Center Circle

Center court line

Three-point line

End of coaching box

Key

THE BASKETBALL COURT

An NBA court is 94 feet long and 50 feet wide (28.6 m by 15.24 m). Nearly all the courts are made from hard maple wood. Rubber mats under the wood help make the floor springy. Each team paints the court with its **logo** and colors. Lines on the court show the players where to take shots. The diagram on the left shows the important parts of the NBA court.

Orlando's home, the Amway Center, is a busy place. Along with basketball, fans there have watched hockey, rodeo, wrestling, skating, and motorcycle riding!

GOOD TIMES

The Magic won their first division title in 1995. It was only their sixth season. They won a club-record 60 games the next year. Tracy McGrady set a team record for points against the Washington Wizards in 2004. He scored 62 that day. The Magic won 108–99. The Magic made the playoffs six years in a row starting in 2007.

During the 1995 NBA Finals, Shaquille O'Neal rose up to block this Rockets shot.

Even three on one, the Magic could not stop
James Harden on his high-scoring night.

TOUGH TIMES

The Magic won only 18 games their first season. Soon, Shaquille O'Neal helped them make the playoffs three times. It was tough on Magic fans when O'Neal signed with the Los Angeles Lakers. James Harden scored 60 points for the Houston Rockets against the Magic in 2018. The Rockets won. The Magic missed the playoffs that season for the sixth year in a row.

ALL THE RIGHT MOVES

Shaquille O'Neal was a powerful dunker. He once dunked so hard he brought down the entire basket. Dwight Howard was a great dunker, too. He was the NBA Slam Dunk champ for 2008. Aaron Gordon makes awesome dunks for today's Magic. Sometimes he dunks with one hand. Sometimes he jams with two. Sometimes he spins and throws it down.

Did O'Neal really break the basket? Yes! In a 1993 game, he made a slam and grabbed the rim. He was so strong, the basket and backboard fell to the floor.

Look out below! Aaron Gordon soars high to slam home a basket.

Tracy McGrady was a four-time NBA All-Star while with Orlando.

HEROES THEN

Nick Anderson was the Magic's first college draft pick. He played more games for the team than anyone else. **Center** Shaquille O'Neal was the NBA Rookie of the Year in 1993. Tracy McGrady was a big-time scorer. He led the league in scoring twice. Center Dwight Howard's nickname was "Superman." He was an all-star six years in a row.

HEROES NOW

Forward Aaron Gordon does it all for the Magic. He scores. He rebounds. He dishes out **assists**. Evan Fournier is one of the top three-point shooters in team history. Jonathan Isaac is a young forward the Magic are counting on to get better and better. Center Mo Bamba is seven feet (2.13 m) tall. He has really long arms. He is a great shot blocker. Nikola Vucevic is another top "big man" for the Magic.

Nikola Vucevic was born in Switzerland, but went to college in the United States.

Magic Uniforms

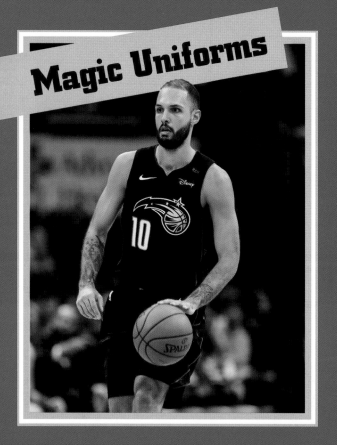

WHAT THEY WEAR

NBA players wear a **tank top** jersey. Players wear team shorts. Each player can choose his own sneakers. Some players also wear knee pads or wrist guards.

Each NBA team has more than one jersey style. The pictures at left show some of the Magic's jerseys.

The NBA basketball is 29.5 inches (75 cm) around. It is covered with leather. The leather has small bumps called pebbles.

The pebbles on a basketball help players grip it.

TEAM STATS

H ere are some of the all-time career records for the Orlando Magic. These stats are complete through all of the 2018–19 NBA regular season.

GAMES

Nick Anderson	692
Jameer Nelson	651

POINTS PER GAME

Tracy McGrady	28.1
Shaquille O'Neal	27.2

ASSISTS PER GAME

Scott Skiles	7.2
Steve Francis	6.5

REBOUNDS PER GAME

Dwight Howard	13.0
Shaquille O'Neal	12.5

STEALS PER GAME

Anfernee Hardaway	1.9
Darrell Armstrong	1.7

FREE-THROW PCT.

Scott Skiles	.892
Darrell Armstrong	.888

THREE-POINT FIELD GOALS

Dennis Scott	981
Nick Anderson	900

NICK ANDERSON

29

GLOSSARY

assists *(uh-SISTS)* passes that lead directly to a basket

center *(SEN-ter)* a basketball position that plays near the basket

drought *(DROWT)* going without something for a period of time

expansion team *(ex-PAN-shun TEEM)* in sports, a team that is added to an existing league

forward *(FORE-word)* a player in basketball who usually plays away from the basket

logo *(LOW-go)* a team or company's symbol

playoffs *(PLAY-offs)* games played between top teams to determine who moves ahead

rivalry *(RY-vuhl-ree)* when two people or groups compete for the same thing

tank top *(TANK TOP)* a style of shirt that has straps over the shoulders and no sleeves

unique *(yoo-NEEK)* one of a kind

FIND OUT MORE

IN THE LIBRARY

Anderson, Josh *Orlando Magic.*
Calgary, AB: Weigl Publishers, 2017.

Big Book of Who: Basketball (Sports Illustrated Kids Big Books). New York, NY: Sports Illustrated Kids, 2015.

Whiting, Jim. *The Orlando Magic.*
Mankato, MN: Creative Paperbacks, 2017.

ON THE WEB

Visit our website for links about the Orlando Magic:
childsworld.com/links

Note to Parents, Teachers, and Librarians: We routinely verify our Web links to make sure they are safe and active sites. So encourage your readers to check them out!

INDEX